I0840976

WORK OR SMERK

by Karen Kellock Ph.D.

Manual for Superior Men

A complete theory based on Einstein physics,
Political Psychology, Systems Theory
and Archetypal Psychiatry.

FORMULA

All success attraction
All disease obstruction
All recovery elimination

You must fast on all three

OBSTRUCTIONS:

People
Habit
Food

WORK OR SMERK

Work on yourself or smirk with the rabble never growing just getting more unstable.   Trauma is in every cell so get that stuff out, work on this *catastrophe*. Why did they abuse you? Because they're toxic, abusive and mentally unstable too. Seek peace of mind regardless of whether you get closure, which is usually futile. It may take a lifetime to go from barely surviving to fully thriving so go gently. You can't change the gossip/what they say about you--just chill out man, that's all you can do.

WHY FRIENDS WILL HATE YOU

SUDDENLY THEY'RE ALL GONE
SUDDENLY THEY HATE YOU
JUST BECAUSE YOU DID IT
EXPECT THE STING
THEY WERE JUST A SCAFFOLD
YOU USED TIME WISELY
THEY LACK YOUR SELF-RESPECT
AN UNDEFINABLE HATRED
YOU TOOK ACTION, THEY DIDN'T
WINNING IS NOT EASY
YOU HAVE A DIFFERENT ENERGY
BUT FROM FRIENDS AND FAMILY?
EVERY TIME YOU FEEL IT
GOD HATES THE WICKED EVERY DAY
THEY LEAVE YOU FEELING EMPTY
THE ROCKY ROAD TO SUCCESS
THANK GOD FOR THE BAD PAST
THE BAD PAST MAKES YOU GREAT
SLEEPLESS NIGHTS
LOOK TO THE HEAVENS
SUFFERINGS ARE STEPPING STONES
LIVE LIKE A JOCKEY
FRUITS AND SOUPS
VOTE FOR A RESTORED AMERICA

WHY FRIENDS WILL HATE YOU

Our biggest haters are people we used to know. It's hard to accept but it's the truth from below.

SUDDENLY THEY'RE ALL GONE

When you've done something to set yourself apart you are hated by friends and family: it's fated.

You make em feel less, threatening their peace of mind and reality. It's hard to take but your fate see.

You can't believe it but they're all gone. It's just another obstacle on your way to success/fame son.

You've changed so much and on a higher frequency it's like a live wire and they escape your matrix see.

It's weird but predictable. It's like they never knew you and it's surrealistic-- and you feel horrible.

If you know what to expect, and can deal with it without fret, you can get thru this stage of the Elect.

Just accept you're like another race/species now and they've been cut off from knowing you, wow!

SUDDENLY THEY HATE YOU

At first you think it's jealousy or spite but it's goes beyond that--it's like a thief in the night.

It's a huge insurmountable gulf now. Your success angers them and it's simply irretrievable bro'.

You thought they'd be happy for you but instead you meet a brick wall and a huge mystery too.

WHY FRIENDS WILL HATE YOU

You feel lonely by this huge rejection but look ahead to the millions who will now love you darlin'.

The difference in vibration is a great spiritual thing and there is no meeting them again on anything.

Perhaps if money's involved they'll hang around, this happened to Elvis with his high school throng.

JUST BECAUSE YOU DID IT

Just because you focused on your own life and did great things it's enough to rattle old friends see.

See it & expect it, that's all you need to overcome it. Laugh at the predictability of it, even love it.

It made me sick when it happened to me but seeing the global pattern I was relieved–I felt freed.

Many as-yet unrecognized geniuses couldn't take it and fell over it, losing the gold ring again, shit!

If they can't take it let em be, the lazy wanna-bes. Let em go and open to your wonderful destiny.

Whether it be jealousy or envy, don't confuse yourself see. Open to a wonderful future not misery.

When you start to see results of your hard labor that's when this stuff starts up, being left forever.

EXPECT THE STING

Expect it sister, that takes the sting out quicker. Predict it brother, it makes your strong and clever.

But you feel so alone! I know, but is it any harder than anything else you've done and known?

WHY FRIENDS WILL HATE YOU

It's just another obstacle, like lifting weights until you're in pain. Think of it that way to fully gain.

Here you expected a reward for your work and instead you are punished by your own, the jerks!

It's like the last test of your character and strength. See it that way, endure: you're got what it takes.

So they left you right at the end, do you really want these flimsy, jealous, insecure friends?

THEY WERE JUST A SCAFFOLD

They were just a scaffold for support while you grew to be king. Once finished they're removed see.

Once it's undeniable you've grown they can't even look at you or hear your name, that's how it is bro'.

Every great has been thru it & passed the test. It's just a pin prick in the whole scheme, the very last.

But it hurts! I know, but no more than everything else you've been through or sacrificed to grow.

They broke your trust--that hurts the most. But welcome to the human race, they're ALL lost.

You're gonna have friends who will love and admire you, who encourage you more not make you blue.

They pretend you don't even exist. That's a new twist that feels so belittling but friend, just persist.

When you have untouchable, undeniable energy pressing forward in life they just hate you, aye.

You're supposed to be part of the crowd, going with the stream, To be so inward just seems mean.

WHY FRIENDS WILL HATE YOU

You keep doing better and better due to your mindset. That's all it is but they sure don't have that.

They basically see it as you won, and they lost. That's the gist and they don't like you being boss.

YOU USED TIME WISELY

You used your time wisely while they just flitted it away, socializing and thinking THAT was the way.

They say certain things but they don't really mean it. They are flimsy that way so you rejected it.

They relied on handshakes and connections while you worked night and day making corrections.

The tough are direct, stoic and solid. The weak rely on manipulation and other social methods.

While they were out there partying you were inside practicing, thinking, planning and preparing.

Now they want what you have but aren't willing to do the things you did to get it, they're just mad.

The losers are just gonna hate. They don't know what love, respect and admiration is all about ok.

THEY LACK YOUR SELF-RESPECT

They don't have the self-respect coming from work so when you do better they just hate of course.

You're on a completely different wave length and they're not that. That they hate, it's as simple as that.

It's hard for you to conceive that would make old friends and family enemies but that's it see.

WHY FRIENDS WILL HATE YOU

Not everybody wins: an obvious fact but the basis of hate coming to you so don't be a sad sack.

You created a life they wanna live themselves. It doesn't matter all the work you did as busy elves.

They just see your big house and new car, not the work hours while staying away from bars.

It's the people you used to know: they're the ones who can't accept your new achieved life bro'.

AN UNDEFINABLE HATRED

They hate you with a hatred that cannot be defined or explained, for all the reasons above ok.

It just angers them. Their ego takes such a HIT at the person you've become it nearly kills em.

The losers actually feel entitled to what you have so their ego takes a massive hit, truly rattled.

They just WANT it all but never take action. You take action, you're a go-getter and get traction.

While they're off taking cruises and vacations you're in here, working with exaction and dedication.

YOU have taken massive action, locked in for years and even decades--but STILL they envy you ok.

YOU TOOK ACTION, THEY DIDN'T

You took repeated action while they just thought about it. They dreamed on and even drank over it.

Life went on while they thought about it but never did shit. They're gonna write a book they insist.

WHY FRIENDS WILL HATE YOU

They drank & ate to the beautiful future that never came cuz constraint was not in their nature ok.

They actually hate you because you've done what they thought about doing. What crazy reasoning!

I'm afraid you're dealing with the peasants who never worked just smirked, that's the essence.

Not everyone is destined for greatness. Don't call em peasants just the attitude of lazy masses.

That's just the human world: there's people at the top, the middle and the bottom of the barrel.

WINNING IS NOT EASY

Winning is not EASY. That's why I like it, easy is boring and useless and that's how I view it see.

Winners don't want easy. They wanna make life hard, spice it up and challenge themselves see.

And when they do, and become the man/woman they're meant to be, here comes the hatred see.

In fact, hatred comes before you even get the results. You trying so hard just makes them nuts.

Tackled many things but mastered nothing. You mastered something then went to the next thing.

A master wants to reach the next level. He knows who he is from achieving while blocking the devil.

When things get stagnant and stay the same that's the devil entering in who wants you empty ok.

A master doesn't understand how things get stagnant. He even gets mad when nothing adds up.

WHY FRIENDS WILL HATE YOU

A master's energy wells up to produce SOMETHING while others dream on while doing nothing.

He doesn't get how they can sleep at night being useless. Without climbing life seems pointless.

We're all equipped to make happen whatever we want to happen. It doesn't occur by future fakin'.

No matter how long/what it takes, a master makes it happen and THAT'S when you're hated on.

YOU HAVE A DIFFERENT ENERGY

You have a different energy, you're just on FIRE! How distinct you are from energy thieves and liars.

You're locked into an entirely new dimension. Tho' they go to the gym they're still locked out son.

They get instant results but stop doing it. They brag on what they did but then it halts, forgetting it.

They can't stay in it for long enough. They make a stab at it then fluff off, they don't have the stuff.

They can't do the reps enough to get what they want and that my friends is what it's all about.

There's many just acting funny too and you can't trust them either Sue. Escape the scene, whew!

BUT FROM FRIENDS AND FAMILY?

Some are your friends or family. They're low key enemies because they're just acting funny.

Something's just not right with the person. You can feel it and see it, just trust your instincts: intuit.

WHY FRIENDS WILL HATE YOU

Get set to get that feeling a lot from those who low key hate you. Trust it cuz this will protect you.

You don't trust them and know something's up. You are skeptical and that brings you luck!

When you feel those vibes towards certain people you know you gotta hater on your hands bro'.

It's not something you're paranoid about it's something you know for a fact so leave him out!

EVERY TIME YOU FEEL IT

EVERY TIME you feel that, it doesn't matter who it is: family or past friends are the culprits sis.

Only if you support them will they stick around and flatter you son, but is this your idea of fun?

Otherwise they're gonna do you dirty. Get as far away as you can to keep your reputation shiny.

They're stalkin' and talkin' about you. Get away so they've nothing to gossip about, or be blue.

They freeze up when they see you cuz they know what they're doing. Recall that when rejecting.

They have to smear you name cuz their ego can't handle the man or woman you're becoming ok?

In the end it just makes you stronger as you rise up and they inevitably fall: that's the matrix bro'.

GOD HATES THE WICKED EVERY DAY

Stop saying God loves everyone cuz Psalms 11 says He hates the wicked every day, just sayin'.

WHY FRIENDS WILL HATE YOU

God is separating us from wicked people: those allowing demons in from sins and evil.

There's either one or two things in us: the Holy Spirit or spirits. It's never empty, just think on this.

We did everything to fit in with people. We drank, we smoked, we laughed at dirty jokes.

You meet up with old friends and they're filled with it. They admire the evil and just don't get it.

THEY LEAVE YOU FEELING EMPTY

They leave you feeling empty, depressed and confused. That's spirits in em and it affected me too.

One with the Holy Spirit leaves you feeling light, happy and RELIEVED. That's God in them see.

They admire creepy people if admired by the world. That's a clear sign to get away fast girl.

A separation of elements is occurring. A clean slate from ALL these people you were admiring.

Some are so dense they marry just because the other has an audience. To me it's so obvious.

They think evil, silly and stupid things. A friend of the world is enemy of God but your heart sings?

Separate and pray for them. God wants all to come to Him but it's preceded by separation.

I'm sick of the news. I prefer old movies from the fifties not these constant repetitions and ads too.

Separation from everything prior is lonely at first but then you're glad as He removes the curse.

WHY FRIENDS WILL HATE YOU

THE ROCKY ROAD TO SUCCESS

As a diamond shines cuz it was cut by friction, success was preceded by trouble and problems.

Gold cannot be purified without fire. You're a queen cuz you learned from thieves, users and liars.

You're not a success from motivational lectures & seminars but from emotional torture & wars.

If we didn't get it from mamas we learned it from hard knocks: treason, betrayals, the dishonest.

All great success sprung from deep canyons of pain. It refined us to gold with guts for great gain.

I didn't get tough from books but from being taken by crooks when lovebombing was all it took.

THANK GOD FOR THE BAD PAST

Don't bemoan the bad past for that was what it took to make you the best and now having a blast.

No one could teach you for you knew it all. So a mean narc became your best teacher, that's all.

For spiritual fitness and joy, thank God for lessons tho' they came from a sadistic man/mean boy.

No one could teach you for "people are good" you thought. Do you see the light now, or not?

The complexion of the whole country is changing cuza men like that, yet you loved that dirty rat?

THE BAD PAST MAKES YOU GREAT

Many can't get over a bad past, never seeing it would make em great with success that lasts.

WHY FRIENDS WILL HATE YOU

You experiment and fail, try harder and fail harder. Then success comes from God your Rewarder.

We try and fail, try and fail as the cycle repeats to no avail until we finally hit gold on a grand scale.

It's our public humiliations which teach us best lest we never stop cringing over the failed test.

It's our embarrassments and faux pas teaching us dignity lest we never forget our little sillies.

We walked a mile to save a penny and boar the criticisms of society to become great see.

We were humiliated by chumps staying down as grunts to finally come freshly endowed to the front.

The best leaders had faces pushed in the mud by inferiors to learn to have mercy/to be tender.

So you got drunk and went to class in your pajamas. Learn to laugh off these valuable traumas.

SLEEPLESS NIGHTS

For great success spend sleepless nights on your desk or wash cars to exist but still you persist.

We had to fight our close ones or walk on roads less taken without applause nor comfort man.

These sad events were essential to succeed though experience was a hard teacher see.

They gave us the hard test first and the lesson after but in the eyes of success our life was better.

Every time you were dumped, every heartbreak you lumped made you better to be loved.

WHY FRIENDS WILL HATE YOU

You may have lost your family or they moved away. People don't stay together like before ok.

LOOK TO THE HEAVENS

Look to the heavens, He's your mainstay. This brings enlightened happiness tho' you're blue today.

Get out in the sunshine, that lightens depression. See the broader universe and feel glad son.

Every insult, everyone who rocked the boat, every humiliation or word misspoke made you gold.

In the eyes of the successful experiences made them better not bitter. Careful if you are the latter.

Our sufferings were necessary trials to test, hurt, cut or embarrass us so we shine like diamonds.

Before becoming successful we must suffer since it's based on taking risks which invite failures.

SUFFERINGS ARE STEPPING STONES

Sufferings are stumbling blocks which strengthen us to convert them to stepping stones like Kellock's.

For years I was embarrassed and shocked at my behavior but now I see I was just rarer.

I stood out so they gossiped like I was rare. That's the pattern of a stigmatized, they're in the glare.

Can you deal with it? Can you transmute cringy self-consciousness to fame and live with it?

Read the book "Stigma" to see the social dynamics surrounding it, how they make so much more of it.

LIVE LIKE A JOCKEY

WHY FRIENDS WILL HATE YOU

Of all the things making me happiest with bliss, eating way less is it but overeating blocks this.

Mashed potatoes with butter tasted like heaven but I was so stuffed it was hell even with oxygen.

Fruit and soup, that's my new motto. I'm happiest being light and quick by maintaining weight low.

I can't eat like others and remain a dynamo. I'm in a class by myself and I've learned this bro'.

FRUITS AND SOUPS

Fruit, soup and occasional dips. Just a bite of this or that but no alcohol ever, not even a sip.

How badly I wanted success determined how constrained I became in eating far less.

Eat like royalty, a queen or king. That means eating next to nothing not the opposite [how it seems].

While they're gorging like pigs you are set apart by your constraint and how CLASSY it all is!

It's not just about gaining weight, I feel a cement block in my gut and that's a failure out the gate.

It's not vanity that keeps my weight down, it's wanting to be like a jockey which success depends on.

It makes em mad this kind of thinking. Don't you just want attention? [They're always accusing].

VOTE FOR A RESTORED AMERICA

Biden is a mean liar who opened the border, botched the Afghan war and destroyed the dollar.

WORK OR SMERK

SPIRIT OF LONELINESS
VISION IS THE SOLUTION
MARRY YOUR VISION
DOING GOD'S WORK
MARRY THE CREATIVE ACT
JOY-BASHING THOUGHT INTRUSION
BEING CONTENT IS AN ACHIEVEMENT
MAKE LAUGHTER A MUST
TOXIC UNHEALTHY PEOPLE ABUSE
GETTING CLOSURE
TOXIC PEOPLE DON'T SELF-REFLECT
INAUTHENTIC PEOPLE STAY DULL
SPACE EXPOSES THE MEAN FLAKES
FORGET CLOSURE WITH LIARS
DON'T SEND THE LETTER
THE BODY KEEPS THE SCORE
WORK OR SELF OR SMIRK TO ADAPT
EVIL FLOURISHES THEN MOWED DOWN
THE JEZEBEL SPIRIT DIVIDES
CYCLE OF ENEMY UP THEN DOWN
RETIREES GETTING DRUNK DAILY
GOLDEN OR DECLINING YEARS?
ALCOHOL: FORGOTTEN IN ETERNITY
YOU EARNED WHAT YOU GOT
EXHAUSTION FROM THEIR CHAOS
THANK GOD FOR YOUR ENEMIES
PRESUMPTUOUS UNASKED-FOR ADVICE
ANOSOGNOSIA: CAN'T SEE YOU'RE SICK
HYPERSENSITIVES IN LIBERAL ENVIRONMENTS
SUBSTITUTE GUILT/SHAME THOUGHTS
THEY KNOW THEY'RE RIGHT THO' WRONG
SCHOOLS ENCOURAGE HOMOSEXUALITY

WORK OR SMERK

THEY'RE WEAK NOT STRONG LIKE THEY THINK
TRAUMA-BASED MIND CONTROL
EVERYTHING STOLEN COMES BACK
THE CURSED CHURCH
LIBS SEEK THE WISDOM OF PAGANS
OUR GREATEST DAYS ARE AHEAD
BE YE SEPARATE!
GOD LOVES CHARMING DIFFERENCES
501C3 CHURCHES ARE UNEQUALLY YOKED
CHRISTIANS EVEN ATTACKED IN THE 70'S
CORRUPTION OF BOYS
50 YEARS OF GLOBALISM REVERSED
ABUSE OK—IT'S JUST THEIR CULTURE
LIBERALISM IS NOW EXTREME AND MEAN
WOMEN CAPTURE MEN
CRUMBLING FAMILIES IS WAR TO THE BRAIN
DOUBLE STANDARDS
STING-SHOTS AND FLIP-FLOPS
LIBERTY LOVERS LOVE THE LORD
WITCHCRAFT INTERSECTS FEMINISM
FEMINISTS COPY MALE DEBAUCHERY
GOOD MARRIAGE IS TOTAL JOY
DEALING WITH DEMOGRAPHIC CHANGE
TRUMPSTERS ARE HATED SO AVOID EM
FORCED US TO BE "SOCIAL" OR INSULT
GROOMED AND GLIB CHANGE-MAKERS
YOU'RE NOT CHOOSING YOU'RE FOLLOWING
SWEET LIL' LADIES OF THE FIFTIES
RACE REALISM IS NOT RACISM
ABOUT YOUR GREAT WORK: PROCEED!
BE NEAT, ORDERLY AND ROUTINED

WORK OR SMERK

SPIRIT OF LONELINESS

You can't be in God's presence and lonely. Get close to God, the spirit of loneliness is blocked.

You may be alone but there's no deficiency when firmly affixed in His presence, believe this.

You can't be in the presence of God and also depressed about the absence of someone else.

The cure for loneliness is focusing on your vision. Stop saying you're lonely, it ends in boredom.

"I'm lonely, I need someone" but honey you're not ready for anyone still steeped in a trauma bond.

If you're not content by yourself you're not qualified to be with anyone else. Put this first.

Marriage won't solve your loneliness and when surrounded by a crowd it just gets worse.

Suicide of famous people comes from emptiness inside. Master your spirit then "fill" with pride.

When powerful people stink they hire out to hide that stink instead of just repenting I think.

Like putting cologne on a sweat: instead of improving she hires out to spin better, no regrets.

VISION IS THE SOLUTION

Focus on your vision. Busy people don't obsess over the absence of others, it's all creation.

WORK OR SMIRK

You should be so in tune with your vision that goals become antidote to loneliness, go head on!

When you have goals & purpose you don't sit around whining about who isn't with you, fussed.

There's no greater turnoff than neediness. If I cave in to you're needing me I lose time and destiny.

Where there is no vision the people perish [means: living without restraint, lines or self-control].

Living a life without vision is like a ship without a rudder always in reaction but never for creation.

A rudderless boat drifts in whatever direction the current takes it. That's you loser, good riddance.

There's too much I'm in pursuit of to sit around whining about who I don't have, vision is my salve.

A pursuit of vision will eradicate thoughts of loneliness. It's glorious, people are encumbrance.

MARRY YOUR VISION

You need to marry your vision. You're single and alone but this will put you solidly on the throne.

I married my vision. I go to bed and wake up with it, it runs my life with daily routines in seclusion.

I write all day and night long, whatever comes through. How would i ever have time to miss you?

When you marry your vision the right spouse will immediately recognize you-- this is most cool.

With a vision you're in your purpose. As long as you're whining about who's not here, you've lost.

WORK OR SMIRK

The right spouse for you can't even recognize you if not in your purpose. He'll run away in disgust.

DOING GOD'S WORK

Be too productive to be lonely. Now the world rushes in demanding your attention, it's a certainty.

God said I want you to write constantly and not for money. I said it's a pleasure to serve, gladly.

I'm a vessel for Your wisdom, a paintbrush in Your hands. Thank you for the chance, I will expand.

Ok God I'll work for nothing. Money's not my goal, pleasing You is and it's a thrill contributing.

If you want me writing all day whatever comes thru I'll do it for You without concern for what accrues.

I don't write for houses and cars but to be better and better until all that stuff just follows.

To the men I knew: Sorry but it makes me sick thinking about you--broken bonds are devil's tool.

God pays me in so many ways. I live in a country mansion in his presence every creative day.

We get lonely when not engaged in self discovery. It's a full time job leaving no time to be lonely.

MARRY THE CREATIVE ACT

I gave up my life and all social contacts for the Creative Act and God rewarded me richly in fact.

Fulfill your vision and both the Creative Act and the reward itself will fall together in a fabric elf!

WORK OR SMIRK

I avoid people day and night and write, write, write. God is rewarding me with things so out of sight!

I don't write to finish this or that part. I write as my work this morning cuz I do it for the Lord.

I'd be happy then my thoughts would take me into a dark, deep place. This is very poor management.

I write all day on two catnaps and meals are light. I'm content cuz it's a call of God on my life.

Tho' your bad actions triggered their rejection, God bashed em anyway seeing your future son.

JOY-BASHING THOUGHT INTRUSION

Most importantly, manage your thoughts. A great day can be suddenly ruined as they interrupt.

You're high as a kite then your thoughts bring you down into depression. Manage this blight son.

I'm so sick of the outer world I'm gonna turn inward to my soul and just the household members.

That's my great fortune as a woman: the home's is my first consideration and I love it man.

You're not going to get to your goal without managing your thoughts not being a rudderless boat.

To manage thoughts you gotta be fine with whatever position life puts us in. Crucial solution.

I don't look at this work or my situation thru my thoughts about it but rather God's call on it.

BEING CONTENT IS AN ACHIEVEMENT

WORK OR SMIRK

He put me in a shack/ghost town and I was happy with it: history! He put me in a mansion, beauty!

I have **LEARNED**--learned--to be content in whatever state I am. First in a shack then a mansion.

I loved my tiny shack in the wilderness. I could see forever, just me and God in His absoluteness.

I loved my little shack so much I had to be forcibly extracted to my mansion, imagine that.

We're to bring every thought into captivity--that means not letting it ruin your life suddenly.

We're to cast down imaginations and every high thing exalting itself against God's wisdom.

That's learning to manage your thoughts. This is where self-control comes in and joy follows.

Loneliness is the consequence of our thoughts. Think whatever's true, honest, pure, lovely, just.

MAKE LAUGHTER A MUST

Make laughter a must. When alone the spirit can get crushed but good cheer wipes off the dust.

CHOOSE not to be depressed. Misery is an option but survivors are the only ones thinking like this.

You don't need a therapist for depression or filling you with prescriptions, that's all bull hon'.

You're depressed from what you're eating or cuz you're fat. Self-control will take care of all that.

With God's love your situation is most fortunate, far better than others so thank Him/look up.

WORK OR SMIRK

I felt so guilty for complaining to the Son. When I looked all around my blessings did abound.

God says cheer is healthy bones so I make laughter my priority and also music in happy reverie.

A merry heart doeth good like a medicine but a broken spirit dries the bones. Laugh/party/have fun.

Would-be genius/a dried up spirit has an incapacity for leisure so laugh, party on and don't fear it.

We're all encumbered by a past ruining relationships. Don't let it, look forward instead.

When you find funny things save em and go back to em. Buy whole series for the best laugh makin'.

Do high walls equal high disgust? Probably, thinking of everything barbarians can do to us.

TOXIC UNHEALTHY PEOPLE ABUSE

Work on your self or smirk to get along with rabble while never growing just getting more unstable.

Trauma is physically enmeshed in every cell of our body. Get that stuff out, work on this catastrophe.

Well, why did they abuse you? Well because they're toxic, abusive and mentally unstable too.

Seek peace of mind within YOU--regardless of whether you get closure, which is usually futile.

It may take a lifetime to go from barely surviving to fully thriving [after that family] so go gently.

Choose to heal [from them] on your own terms--be the CEO of your divine self, *away* from them.

You can't change the news/what they say about you. Just chill out man, that's all you can do.

GETTING CLOSURE

"Closure" is not a prerequisite for healing since it depends on the sick system/the unrelenting.

It happens: the one cutting contact with the entire family system due to one narcissistic sibling.

When one is finally done the family will band together with the narcissist against this one.

Of course he walks away despite losing contact with the parents who the narcissist controls ok.

Scapegoating one plays out in adulthood in extended families and it's a cruel thing/heartbreaking.

When the siblings only means of survival is distancing they may not see parents for decades see.

Typically you won't get closure in an abusive family showing these lethal characteristics.

Closure: A bringing to an end, a conclusion. Finality or resolution especially after trauma.

Why didn't we receive closure? Because most don't receive the truth nor self-reflect for sure.

TOXIC PEOPLE DON'T SELF-REFLECT

Toxic, psychologically unstable people don't do the work of self-reflection or deep questioning.

Nor does a narcissist care to make positive changes in words, actions or behaviors--so there.

WORK OR SMIRK

Therefore "they" will not be moving forward but YOU my friend have this opportunity to SOAR.

Closure is a final resolution to problem or conflict. It brings relief/return to health after being sick.

In most cases with sibling abuse there are no apologies but there never was healthy transparency.

INAUTHENTIC PEOPLE STAY DULL

They are inauthentic. Thus you'll never get a straight answer and shouldn't expect one either.

All you've had is a web of lies so why a straight answer now? Closure dies where truth is despised.

Without closure we look within. Then we assemble the puzzle and are shocked at the machinations.

Could they get any dirtier, more low down? Yes they could, evil is infinite in these showdowns.

SPACE EXPOSES THE MEAN FLAKES

Suddenly I realized her betrayal had gone on far longer than I ever fathomed, a gossiping demon.

Typically we don't see how bad it was until we go no-contact/have space to mentally investigate.

It took me 15 years to wake up to their gang up and it took me down a rabbit hole of evil setups.

At this point we don't want more [lame excuses or petty lies] in "closure" but just God our Father.

It's better to heal on your own, not relying on "closure" but firm boundaries and moving forward.

FORGET CLOSURE WITH LIARS

WORK OR SMIRK

Forget closure and enter your beautiful transformative pathway giving you final peace and hope.

The need for closure centers around a missing "piece" but we can't get it since they're dishonest.

They lie about anything to keep you outa the loop. You're pegged as a stupe, that's all there is to it.

They will never admit facts and instead deny us our own conscious reality of their cruel impacts.

Instead of "why did they betray us" we walk away--way ahead--with life lessons of amazing depth.

Like a concentration camp victim who'll never trust people again, we've gained similar wisdom.

DON'T SEND THE LETTER

Write a letter but don't send it sister cuz there's still no closure/honesty about this family war.

A sent letter will bring no closure but just more anger or nothing in return--and more lack of closure.

Acknowledge you're back in the driver's seat and they have no control--that era's done/complete.

There was a reason you walked away--from malicious, hateful abusive people, keep that central.

Not one person in the clan would listen to me, they all said I was too sensitive/seeing things.

I could read between the lines or discern double meanings but that was "paranoid" see.

I felt secrecy everywhere. They were discussing me when I wasn't there. I cited the Lord's Prayer.

WORK OR SMIRK

We bounce between angry and sad in stages of grief. Drowning or staying afloat: accept the variability.

After a period of time away we're flooded with triggers and flashbacks--it's a normal response.

THE BODY KEEPS THE SCORE

"The body keeps the score" refers back to epigenetics, cell memory and body-mind connection.

Another way of saying it: Memory is stored in fecal matter [shit] beneath the neck so get rid of it.

Cleanse your memories through colon cleansing. Make your past beautiful, abundant, light again.

If one EATS at memory they become more obdurate see. Fast at em and they disperse to eternity.

With detox the past breaks down like an evil nightmare that scared then disappeared like vapor.

I use fasting and have seen when eating wrong my memories become like tainted songs.

Expand your horizons. Take classes, get creative, go into solitude in nature, thank Jesus the Son.

Realize this is how God wants you: happy and joyful not miserable in the presence of those devils.

The spiritual is the most beneficial. You'll feel emotionally supported and protected on a hill.

On the financial you clearly see the louse. They'd do anything to keep you from your inheritance.

WORK OR SELF OR SMIRK TO ADAPT

WORK OR SMIRK

Work or Smerk: They're FAKING it and that's not in God's groove while we're creating it as He behooves.

They kept dropping by to impose on me, interrupt my work, make me adapt to them: that was liberalism.

They'd come to my home and bring all their friends. The social liberal sees nothing wrong/no offense.

To the liberal generation, the social transcends independence (where the power is). Yak yak, blah blah.

The dam liberal will wreck your privacy every time. That's not his thing, he's a gang social chummy guy.

They're for killing babies, Hillary and debauchery: that's liberal women and that's all I can say.

EVIL FLOURISHES THEN MOWED DOWN

You gotta know that evil will flourish but will be mowed down. It's a biblical promise so just hold on.

If you can endure the fallout from being different before famous you get the reward of world success.

Count on them flourishing first--COUNT on it. For you know their day is coming, that's the pattern.

The herd is built on ENVY. The sage is SAVVY and thus he's well-protected from the masses/happy.

You bring a Jezebel in, you bring devastation upon yourself. Inevitably she'll destroy it all.

Inevitably/inexorably Jezebel needles you, gets others against you, humiliates and ruins you too.

THE JEZEBEL SPIRIT DIVIDES

WORK OR SMIRK

She introduces you to her friends who hate you then she'll mock you later to them, always instigating.

The Jezebel spirit is the serpent and it must divide, conquer, belittle and mock till you're dead.

"Tender loving female spirit" is how it's portrayed--getting a little tenderness in there, but that's insane.

Jezebel spirit divides churches, neighborhoods, families, coffee klatches or any group you care for.

Jezebel SPIRIT is a homesick dread of being carried away in a sea of vicious misjudgment by a jealous twit.

Cuz that's what it's all about: *protection* because human nature is EVIL and that's the Christianity I know.

These imposers can't get to me anymore but due to PTSD memories I feel defensive like they're still here.

It wasn't as bad as a man going off to war. My obstacles were just social but they were horrible.

CYCLE OF ENEMY UP THEN DOWN

Expect them to flourish but then to be killed. See this cycle, it's crucial, and your faith is fulfilled.

Tho' "loving" the Jezebel spirit is mean and divisive and I can't see how you can stand being around it.

First Calvinist principal: UTTER [TOTAL] DEPRAVITY describes human nature even the mature.

So EXPECT it--depravity--and you got it. Even if you have to build a wall and a molt around it.

Ray's a fence but Jimmy was an open sieve allowing it ALL in because he thought that was good.

Women too are woefully naive about evil human nature and tend to trust, to their total displeasure.

Or women in power will tend to trust even criminals since it virtue-signals the redemption of animals.

Don't hanker over people cuz even when you find em they're boring as hell. Attend to God NOW.

RETIREES GETTING DRUNK DAILY

There's nothing interesting about modern people and if they're into alcohol they're empty too.

EMPTY: No emotions, having adapted to falsity for so long they're just dumbed. Alcohol: numbed.

They can't handle the quietude of retirement so get drunk daily. Post-time earlier each day, but it's ok.

I'm so grateful Ray doesn't drink or smoke. He doesn't even watch ballgames all day long, OH!

The rate of alcoholism doubles/triples with retirement. It's ugly since this grand time should be our best.

Alcoholism creeps in insidiously. You start more early and think about it constantly on the way to tipsy.

I wanted it too much. I either over-anticipated first drink or was recovering from yesterday's mistake.

Men are emotionally brittle--can't handle it--so they self-medicate thru alcohol and can't live without it.

Fortunately the physical hangovers were so debilitating I could never drink again, even diluted wine.

A little right-brain herb, fine. But nothing of the left-brain downer type where anosognosia crosses lines.

GOLDEN OR DECLINING YEARS?

If retirement is the apex of our life--the golden years--then why ruin it with alcohol my dear?

It's called Abuse Amnesia as you breaking the no-contact rule activates the trauma bond again you fool.

Alcohol is such a poison hypersensitives can't drink it without results so tragic but sobriety is magic.

A trauma-bonded addicted brain plays tricks and lies--anything for a drink or to be with that guy.

I wake up alive and work all night, so fascinated I look everything up cuz alcohol's not in my life.

A little herb man, but give up the alcohol. This is no way to end it all and you have a life to live ya know.

I don't even know anyone who drinks. What Jimmy put me thru for decades was horrible that fink.

Why I don't like being around em: It's our different views of time. They act like it's gone, I feel it's sublime.

Sobriety is the right-brain cornucopia of all of life coming magically together in an eternal jigsaw puzzle.

ALCOHOL: FORGOTTEN IN ETERNITY

What they saw as wasting time was actually something I was doing which was important for mankind.

The arrogant narcissist with no self-awareness will bring up your sins of years ago, don't let him/GO.

After drinking alcohol I would wake up terrified. It was so awful I'd resume drinking, that's the downside.

And don't take Nyquil or cough medicines. I went out again on Nyquil, it was truly sickening.

I went baseline in the med center after drinking alcohol. I died, came back and Doc said never do that.

There are weak traitors in everyone's family who choose to join the evil side seeking power or likes.

Give her an inch and she will take a mile--that's Jezebel. Give her an edge and you'll wish you were dead.

They wanna gut the economy first then take the guns. With so many new ones it'd be dangerous.

With PTSD the point is not to focus on those toxic events but how you are now with proper defense.

Don't keep going back cuz it makes you feel vulnerable. Re-focus always on your strength now, able.

YOU EARNED WHAT YOU GOT

If you were stupid enough to let them in your life then you deserved what you got. It's jungle life/ROT.

I don't care that someone told you to do it--to be nice. You must defend yourself/ ignore bad advice.

Instead of reliving the memory/feeling fear, refocus on the protections and comforts you have today dear.

You ventured outside your home/what you know and got hurt. Now you've matured, lesson learned.

Women tear down their homes by talking to other men and getting involved on the outside, amen.

When single I wanted to stay home and they castigated me for it--especially the churches did this.

WORK OR SMIRK

STAYING HOME is what people always did you social twits. Your home is a dam mess I'll bet.

What the gross youth don't understand about us oldsters is that we see things and it's truly sickening.

EXHAUSTION FROM THEIR CHAOS

I'm so tired from the chaos you've caused with this gang of losers you call friends so good riddance.

Every woman I knew cut me down to their friends/family to get an army against me all from envy.

I'm talking mother, sisters, aunts, great-aunts. All ruthless gossips about the "one"--the odd girl out.

It's like all women do, hold each other down as they constantly balance forces around them.

They hate upstarts/new girls on the block. What I went thru in a small town was foundation for growth.

When I cut Jezebel loose my world was calm again, free of chaos from flying monkeys or "friends".

THANK GOD FOR YOUR ENEMIES

I learned more from that Jezebel than a library of books. Look at the past this way, it brings you back.

Here I hadn't seen Danny in 30 years and the first thing he does is bring up my sins as if he's all clean.

That's the kind of thing I expect from heathen. All about your sins but never theirs--no self-awareness.

Now I'm looking forward to heaven not backward to you, a nothing/ leaven--of no consequence/demon.

WORK OR SMIRK

You were just my lesson about demons--insidious, tenacious little nobodies who attach on.

Learn to say "I hate your dependency". Don't be supply for his place to stay, washing machine, money.

Don't get too close too fast cuz when you pull back it may get violent. That's the way it is now darlin'

My job is to write these little quips and the strange thing is when I was just a little kid my dad said it!

All about my sins from way back, not about your sins right now of being a whoremonger in fact.

OK: I won't think about what you did in '95 but what I'm doing now in a cozy protected room relieved.

Cuz when I think of how you imposed on me I get angry with adrenalin and dread. I can't have that.

All about my sins from way back but it's all-ok your porn collection and other things acceptable today.

I'm busy escaping a Dunning-Kruger Effect of the severe undertow from dumb people henpecked.

All about my sins from way back but not a word about a lazy wino drinking all day and night in fact.

PRESUMPTUOUS UNASKED-FOR ADVICE

The worst part is presumptuous unasked-for advising when they came with your friend, imposing.

The best advice I can give for protection in the modern world: get married, get a guard, get armed.

I can hear people/women yelling at me, that's all that remains of the old life of all loss/no gains.

WORK OR SMIRK

My new stone garden replacing foliage always looks perfect so I can bask in the sun and think.

Mom would drink all thru the holidays agonizing over the coming get-togethers, what does that say sir?

Why is everything about narcissism now? Cuz since WWII it's all about me/now so it's literally everywhere.

You must find the gem in the trash or after all that pain you'll ruminate over it and never let it go.

If you don't find those benefits in all that pain it'll hurt you for so long and you'll never get rid of it.

It's easier to accept what happened when you realize cruel humans *are* the dangers of being famous.

It happened, you weren't protected enough. But it'll never happen again cuza what you learned from it.

Beta males have mother's identity. That's why it's now so easy for women taking over the republican party.

ANOSOGNOSIA: CAN'T SEE YOU'RE SICK

Anosognosia: Being mentally ill and not knowing it. Going through life in denial but not hiding it.

With anosognosia you wake up to reality years later--like a movie reel of all your insanities and players.

I went into blind denial to save myself while in that impossible situation I'm now waking up to.

The world turned against me, on the potter's wheel. I go into blind denial and now see the movie reel.

The criticisms of the narcissist can be non-verbal or just mental. He seems so nice but you're belittled.

WORK OR SMIRK

Start of relationship: There's so much I wanna tell him. End: He never listens anyway, hell with him.

It's hard seeing past sins but when you know anosognosia is a mental illness you can self-forgive.

What happened in California stayed there. Ray yanked me out one day and that past is now vapor.

HYPERSENSITIVES IN LIBERAL ENVIRONMENTS

Any hypersensitive living in a liberal environment will go crazy unless they see the system/stay steady.

There's so much I wanted to tell you but I soon saw you don't care to know anything at all too.

I was driven subconsciously. Generational curse? Genetic predisposition? Who knows, I'm good now.

I had to forgive myself for being blind. This too is mental illness so it should be easy to do this and go on.

I had to go dense due to the public humiliation and calumny from sisters, mothers, aunts.

For women are BEASTS to each other. They keep you in line far more than men: your sadistic sisters.

Controlling women are mediocre thinkers, mistaking slogans for wisdom they are groupthink-dumb.

Narcissist says "I don't understand" but in explaining it you get hooked back in. Just end it man.

SUBSTITUTE GUILT/SHAME THOUGHTS

SUBSTITUTE guilt and shame thoughts with who you are today and what you learned from the fray.

Always bring the intrusive thoughts forward. Guilt and shame--bring it forward to who you are today.

With time substituting thoughts the past will eventually break down, replaced by a brand new reality.

I loved what the psychologist had to say but when I met his feminist wife I thought: WTF, no way.

What's inside his head? Nothing about me that's what I see, he's onto thee but you are temporary.

Well you've won. I'm gonna retire into total solitude just to get away from you but books are still viewed.

It was so horrible knowing every last one of ya'. Not one person from California will I remember, hah.

SUBSTITUTE GUILT/SHAME FOR WHO YOU ARE TODAY

THIS LITTLE TRICK WILL END THE INTRUSIVE MEMORIES

WHICH IS PTSD FROM THE TRAUMA CAUSED BY ENEMIES.

THEY KNOW THEY'RE RIGHT THO' WRONG

Liberals just know they're right, though they are wrong. LIberalism seems so true, though it's false/they're at fault.

WORK OR SMIRK

They think they're smart but they're not. They think they're chic but they're up a creek/their ideas are rot.

You're a joke, you're not true intellectuals, you're a fraud. But we're still waiting for you to come around.

Baphomet the transgender god of bisexuals is the evil demon worshipped by university "intellectuals".

The level of hate for the joker who was in the Whitehouse ramped up to disgust (never again) for any leftist louse.

The alien crime wave is a nightmare of violence and Trump's gonna deport em all so we finally have quietness.

Not in my lifetime will I ever have to endure liberal "superiors" and I'll never stop thanking God/the Savior.

Some of us had lousy liberals in our families/homes. They ruined everything with their crazy syndromes.

Dear Lord, Father in heaven: We'll never stop thanking you for killing the serpent and removing the leaven!

SCHOOLS ENCOURAGE HOMOSEXUALITY

The schools encouraged our kids to be homosexual! They said it was superior when it's really the devil.

School books became pornography--can you imagine that? This era will go down in history as crap.

Dark, devilish, debauched. That was what we endured for eight years with a faker, an historical blotch.

Poets are higher than writers cuz they have power and that's why dictators hate em/they're disfavored.

To all of you taken in, voting for him: enabling a criminal takeover, turning our great country into a trash bin.

WORK OR SMIRK

Liberals are a disgrace. Your patriot relatives would turn over in their grave if knew you wanted his ugly face!

We're not out of the woods: he's not gone yet--him and his hoods--but God'll get him out cuz He's good.

They're self-serving not giving like you and me. They're a sick club not "love", don't you see?

They are bought not self-taught. They're a blot not something you should want/can't do without.

They went to the "best" schools but learned nothing but the ideology of fools (how to be so cruel).

To liberals it's about how you say it not what you do: smiling and appearing cool while delivering the screws.

Though they were smug now just thugs sweeping it all under the rug. What they put us through: uugghh!

Witchcraft (even Harry Potter) is satanic: like sticking finger into an electric socket--you will be shocked.

Silly liberals will become increasingly irrelevant. What a relief returning to logic after the vitriolic.

America's about admiring the common man, hard-worker/striver. Not this Hollywood/football palaver.

THEY'RE WEAK NOT STRONG LIKE THEY THINK

They're weak not strong like they think. Their ideas are corny, rehashed, mimicked and rinky-dink.

We'll soon be rid of the communist. Just like Castro he'll be gone and we'll be the richest and happiest!

Though we voted out all communists we're still leery and apprehensive that they can still wreck us.

WORK OR SMIRK

Though he's on the way out he's still the devil intent on making trouble. The solution: pray/stay humble.

Castro's death is so symbolic as leftism is imploding all over the world and we SEE the illogic--so evil/toxic.

In 1860, 4 millions slaves were owned by democrats who started the KKK but shifted the blame to us, ok?

Uncertainty of right vs. wrong is moral relativism: bull since the sixties and debunked by us Christians.

Even churches haul em to Harry Potter movies thinking it's all-ok. It's not, it's rot: sickening I say.

The Green Party is a watermelon--green on outside, red on inside: these communists are sweet venom.

Been in Utah 8 months, outa California: lewd and liberal. May be hard to believe but that's typical.

They aren't inclusive so why should I be? If they'd be tolerant I'd be tolerant but that's not happening.

It's natural for body to reject a pathogen harming the body infected--but in Germany you'd be arrested.

For the left, destroying the host (west's society/power) is the goal--always think of that before you vote.

TRAUMA-BASED MIND CONTROL

Extreme abuse is trauma-based mind control and that's the vile cult of Islam that the left extols.

Perhaps opening the gates to Muslims was necessary to re-energize the right with popular support?

God is not done with America: it's the platform so the end time harvest can go forth, so have great mirth.

WORK OR SMIRK

God's gonna purge America of this corruption and illegals will begin to leave right after his inauguration.

A wonderful peace is soon to come over our land and all the west: All because of our guy, the best!

Everyone in the world is watching Trump cuz they know it'll be a domino effect for their country: AH!

Even non-Christians are standing up for what's right. Donald Trump is a trigger for everyone in this fight.

ISIS brings panic like it's the end, but no! it is the beginning and the end of Lucifer's sinning.

The biggest corruption resulted from the church's political correctness: aiding invaders/creating a mess.

Obama's legacy will be purged by the stroke of Trump's pen.

Trump will shut gates Obama opened and open those he shut.

Through this man the seeds America has sown since birth will now come to harvest and it'll be so marvelous!

America will prosper like never seen before in the history of the nation. Look up, thank God for our mansion!

America sowed seeds throughout the world: food, clothing, money. Now it's time for our harvest, honey!

EVERYTHING STOLEN COMES BACK

Everything stolen from America is coming back. A seven-fold return after the damage from Barrack!

Evil globalists have the tech to ruin us with disasters but God said no: it's not My plan, I've got The Man.

501c3 has decimated our churches/made them worthless.

WORK OR SMIRK

501c3 churches are censored churches. That's the devil as the state encroaches against God's riches.

There is no tax-exempt gospel. That's censorship and false religion--no redemption--and bitter pill.

Kids don't know right vs. wrong or how government works so are easy prey to ideas of communist perks.

Seek patriotic pastors or disaster.

Surely a present makes a wise man mad and a bribe destroys the heart. Eccl. 7:7

Don't twist judgement for a bribe blinds the eyes of the wise and perverts the works of the righteous. Deut. 16:19

Take a bribe and all discernment is lost along with revelations, perverting the works of the righteous.

These churches aren't intentionally corrupt they're just blind from taking a bribe.

1964 Prayer was taken out of schools and churches were silent so they didn't lose tax status: hellish hiatus.

THE CURSED CHURCH

Since it was silent over abortion the church is under a curse.

As the true church we want independence from government intrusion as that was the Christian-erosion.

We can't have the church connected to the failed system (of making money) because the results are ugly.

The churches for 62 years: Tax exempt status and a bribe for keeping your mouth shut and to lie.

WORK OR SMIRK

They'll be out of power and I love rubbing it in as we've had to deal with liberalism in the school system.

I was a liberal by default--we all were. We thought we were all-good because of it—how weird!

Liberals adore dictators. Progressives love how they "get things done" instead of dealing with public opinion.

As much as I want to be with people nothing's as good as being alone because that's on my throne.

Walls change everything whether a nation or a home. No need to roam/no adaptation to syndromes.

If you have walls it doesn't matter if you hate the neighbors, you can just forget about em and their disfavor.

You must take threats seriously. Fence up, lock up, board up, gear up, arm up and avoid tragedy.

College brainwashing is a form of psycho-warfare by instilling shame for being themselves: white, that's all.

We gotta purge the academics. They are the worst traitors of all, in fact they're the ones steering it.

LIBS SEEK THE WISDOM OF PAGANS

Things have changed and liberals are shocked, dismayed and irrelevant. Some may seek you to explain it.

What liberalism has always done is seek the wisdom of pagans. Imagine that: sinking to such low stations.

They love the earth: "interplanetary coming together". Behind it is occult spirituality: demons/stormy weather.

Paganism is no longer called "new age" but rather "progressive spirituality" and it's globalism/not ok.

WORK OR SMIRK

Modernity is a worldview on the nature of existence which is thoroughly pagan.

The entire worldview since the hippies (we are one B.S.) is based on paganism. The solution: two-ism.

Paganism seeks to eliminate guilt but that's necessary for the fall into humility and then being rebuilt.

Power of rationalization drives the culture war. They must lambast/overstate to enforce viewwith make sure.

A yes person is a miserable watered down wasteland. He's lost his Self so needs boring events planned.

I messed up when reflecting my generation. I grew up when transcending them and all their friends.

God through Trump will expose the backroom deals of the court, a great light to the whole world once more.

OUR GREATEST DAYS ARE AHEAD

Cheer up America, your greatest days are ahead of you--as God raises up an army to fight for you!

The illness is characterized by denial so how'd I know I was wrong but years later I felt remorse over the trials.

Puppy knows mommy has two sides so he doesn't act to bring that out-- that's how God works, no doubt.

The new age goes mainline when you hear them say "I'm spiritual but I'm not religious": that's the occultists.

The issue of sexuality is used as a battering ram against Western culture to destroy it altogether.

You either worship the creation (in infinite ways) or the Creator who is blessed forever: simplify with the latter.

WORK OR SMIRK

One-ism destroys God's blessings and light totally. It's him not we're "one" like we're all God--how silly.

Hindu means "not two"--formed in opposition to a separate God discerning good/evil and loving me and you.

One-ism says you're God--but you don't look/smell like Him: the most absurd generation ever been.

Hindu is committed to breaking the distinction between God and man, making it all one: How boring and bland.

Hindu wants to bring God down to man at his will. But God blesses who He wants, He sees who steals/kills.

Paganism—one-ism--is joining opposites in bath/locker rooms and here we see the insanity in full bloom.

If God is in us all-one, who's gonna bless us? God is separate so He blessed me with things precious.

If you wanna save society preach two-ism: It's not about being "nice" but pleasing God/repenting of vice.

BE YE SEPARATE!

Because she loved Him as separate, holy and superior, He extravagantly blessed her as His dear.

Two-ism not one-ism: I wanna worship God as separate so He can bless and shed His light on me!

One-ism/paganism has taken over our culture for 50 years. See the signs and return to God in good cheer.

If you wanna make it in life, work and please God. For He has plans to prosper and not to hurt you though you're "odd".

A pagan worldview is based on fantasies which get increasingly weirder but to which we're forced to adhere.

WORK OR SMIRK

Hindu means "not two" but two there are and thank you God it's true: you're separate from an evil herd.

Look out for pagan terms: "denial of binaries, discovering non-dual reality, joining dichotomies/opposites."

Preach two-ism and God will reward you greatly for bringing the focus back on Himself, the All Mighty.

Worship creation (in infinite ways) or love the Creator one way, all day: That's the way to high pay.

Unlike the kids, a genius can never view things through the social prism. End up alone, whatever, amen.

I can condense all this cuz I know the difference between God and me, or me thinking I'm God with out Thee.

The fall: A childhood lost, an adulthood gained and a journey into maturity while being caned.

Ask em "why wouldn't you want someone to be good?" and they're theory falls apart--can't defend, no heart.

Holy means separate. Set apart, playing an important part, sanctified by God with gifts infinite.

Pagan Gods are a mere extension of humanity and they are homosexual uniting opposites he and she.

GOD LOVES CHARMING DIFFERENCES

God is all about charming differences not boring and militant homogenization or skittish similitude.

Why do crazy liberals love systems of slavery and push them so haughtily? They know nothing of reality.

Proven but when you mention it they'll come against you for saying it: they aren't mature enough to take it.

This will go down as the sickest/most perverted generation even beyond Hitler's at least they had genders.

Liberals are perverts. Don't tell me this is always how it's been. We were a decent country back then.

Liberals are about including but I'm about dividing: attacking heresies, mythologies and false ideologies.

501c3 opens the door to the counterfeit spirit--that's when in church you don't like it, even fear it.

Five percent of churches are not under the money system so they are the remnant soon to be eminent.

Anyone who says Christians shouldn't vote (partake in our system) is helping Satan: we must resist him.

I'm a Christian who never went to church--could it be because it was part of what I sensed had emerged?

If church is like the society I'm escaping by going to church, what a letdown as God will never come first.

What comes first in the false church? Being social, "loving" people but not God's power/shunning evil?

For victory there are things to do on our end: Intercede, pray, assert, expose, make Christian friends.

501C3 CHURCHES ARE UNEQUALLY YOKED

A 501C3 church is unequally yoked to government, Islam, wicca, Satan, Planned Parenthood/pro-choice.

People really mourn when the wicked rule. For a lesson in Civics these last 8 years were the best school.

The false church marked by liberal drift is now taking down crosses/letting muslims in as if they fit.

WORK OR SMIRK

I'll never stop talking/thinking about the Obama years: the daily trauma and disappointment, and the fears.

Obama years taught us about government, tyranny, globalism, liberalism and the new age generation.

Who knew the value of freedom until it was lost? Who knew what tyranny was before a tyrant was boss?

The Obama years weren't only scary but also dirty. Dark perversions, unheard of things, revulsions.

That whole entitled generation of leftists politicians were hawkish, nasty, dirty, whorish, brutish, outlandish.

Conservatives couldn't get tenure, we were looked down on by globalist pawns, arrogant though dumb.

There were no conservatives lecturing on campus and if so you had to have several armed guards. Hard.

For 8 years the smart had to endure insults from young upstarts calling us "stupid, bigot"--with no heart.

The leftist politicians (friends of Barry O) dressed fashionably chic--did that make them seem smart, ya think?

It started in the sixties, a 50 year war: changes hard to endure but it amped up and now popped, for sure.

We never knew how dirty leftism got until it culminated in Obama's reign of terror/commie fervor.

CHRISTIANS EVEN ATTACKED IN THE 70'S

Even in the 70's we were attacked in colleges for being Christian or conservative, seen as silly and foolish.

I've been attacked by feminists for my words. They yelled and even hit me if no one was around to observe.

WORK OR SMIRK

Hippyism came to it's ugly head and hit glitches but now they're digging in to enforce will of witches.

You talk about ugly and dark--what the kids have done for decades and we enabled it "it's all ok".

The declension into chaos and dissension was so gradual we just got dense but now--wow! awakened at last!

False church always declines through one-ism. All of them--when the two-ists leave/never come again.

They were so stiff-necked and haughty, so mean if you didn't agree, so social while you were a rare anomaly.

Liberals don't seem to be changing or waking up but rather digging in--perhaps that's the way with sin?

Liberals use obscenities--"F" talk to increase their base with losers I guess. Why else speak in a filthy mess?

It is so shocking to hear an "expert" use the F word--but it's common and they insist it's no problem.

Sometimes F talk gets a laugh, sometimes it doesn't go over at all and the result is rejection/it's rough.

It's definitely crossing a line, then compelled to increase it to justify it and that's how all sin works, believe it.

CORRUPTION OF BOYS

The corruption of boys is the greatest delight in the homosexual pagan heart all through history (creates misery).

If they took 'f**kin' out they wouldn't be saying anything: those dumb nuts from the crazy left wing.

Liberals wish to banish us as a country. They're globalists and that means no-borders and tyranny.

WORK OR SMIRK

It's time to stop turning us into global barracks--we're a right to be different. Vladimir Putin, love 'im.

And to think I was brought up/baptized in the Methodist church, haven for heretics, homosexual, /illegal aliens.

Darkness ain't about skin color. It's dirty, horrible, ungodly, devilish squalor yet a "constitutional scholar".

It's hard to believe it's the churches causing all the trouble, taking in a cult that hates us/of the devil.

We in the right brain are seen as unreliable. What we see as productive puttering they see as unviable.

For those who are called "irresponsible" let me ask you one thing: Do you take care of your animals?

While he was playing golf and spending our mint on vacations we were suffering all his regulations.

Our hopes and aspirations will never again go on deaf ears as they were by a queer, think of that dear.

We're gonna have so much money, we're gonna celebrate and party cuz we're free for eternity, so happy.

50 YEARS OF GLOBALISM REVERSED

A populist reversed 60 years of globalism--amazing.

We worried for 8 years, of course we're tired. Anyone is when dominated by thieves, traitors and liars.

The main media hates American people, works for global elites and is covering up a satanic pedophile ring.

I guess it's best to just party for 40 days and nights until The Man gets in to clean up the terrible blight.

Get this to avoid having the blues: The main news is the fake news, the fake news is the main news.

Are you with the herd of socially hypnotized mal-adaptants, liberals, neo-cons or false churchist get-alongs?

Watch entry points to the devil and his demons. What you do, watch, experience and let in are some reasons.

Trump said he would expose all of em not just the queen of the Satanic Worldwide Pedophile Ring.

Being delusional doesn't make you a winner, it means you've been conned. That's no great identity, c'mon!

Look up, look UP then LOOK UP.

Keep looking UP all day and night thanking God He removed the blight.

Quitting your church: Where is that line--when they remove crosses/change to mosques--what is the sign?

The Catholic church was infiltrated by pedophile rings and that's how they're controlled: they're framed, cold.

ABUSE OK—IT'S JUST THEIR CULTURE

Muslim TV gives tips on how to apply makeup over abuse scars. Liberals say "it's ok--it's just their culture".

Trump is talking $1 gas and already this has come to pass!

Why does Obama shower love on our enemies? Castro is liberal chic. Ted Cruz

Why does the left make excuses for monsters like Castro? To maintain identity, he'd become a symbol.

There's an impulse on the left to defend totalitarianism and it makes me so nervous about them.

The most important word is no. It clears the way for the highest in your day so don't say Yes, no pains to allay.

WORK OR SMIRK

ISIS calls for random knife attacks but still the libtards want open borders even the kids and college hacks.

Then the players would cry during our anthem cuz they knew how blessed they were to be here, amen?

The truth is stranger than fiction: It's surrealistic as events unfold in this, the second American Revolution.

The loudest isn't the majority so don't worry. Just a little while longer and we'll have victory/they'll be sorry.
Mean leaders start big wars when they're about to be overthrown and Hillary's the worst ever known.

It makes me sick to hear them actually equate Donald with that pervert. He's a prince but they want her.

Sex crimes with children/child exploitation: That's the worst but not to the herd which accepts abortion.

Our culture's already made dense through abortion-acceptance and thus there isn't more shock/uproar.

Accepting the unacceptable has made us dense: Once the conscience is gone we're a moral dunce.

LIBERALISM IS NOW EXTREME AND MEAN

Liberalism, based on a false premise, became more inveterate and extreme so now we're a sewer and mean.

For anyone who doubts Trump (due to hype) just listen to his speeches. If still in doubt I'm speechless.

Puritanism: a reaction to 18th c. debauchery and that accounts for American decency, until recently.

How does this corruption happen? 1 an uneducated public 2 no term limits 3 a bought off/criminal media.

WORK OR SMIRK

Going against the grain is the way to be free. Constructive anger immediately brings creativity.

He's a military vet with cancer. Give him a break when you ask a question and get an angry answer.

Smart man: The Art of the Deal. First, you salvage. Second, you're savage.

They love Hillary and wanna kill babies. I say take back the vote from these creepy so-called ladies.

Art of the Deal: Fire a person a day if not quite good enough. That's why he's the best/takes no guff.

Wonderful president lovin' on Houston--this is salve on our wounds not salt like fake news is tellin'

Our own media rooting for North Korea against our president? Incredible but that's how they do it.

They may be brainwashed/out of control but still a reality: they mean business and are hard/cold.

Lower IQ means lower impulse control, more in the moment--tastes good while nutrition is absent.

Come unglued when strategies don't work but because they've been brainwashed, can't relearn.

WOMEN CAPTURE MEN

She dresses provocatively so that the male stops thinking, is sexually aroused and then captured.

Sex, then a noose around his neck for 18 years: child support (or jail if he fails) so men: stay aware.

Hypersexuality is the downfall of Western civilization.

The usual postmodern mosaic is a stitched-together family frankenstein and it's destroying society.

WORK OR SMIRK

History shows niceness gets you killed.

In fatherless homes the girl may hypersexualize and the boys aggressive.

Japanese families stay together and you don't see girl hypersexuality or boy aggressiveness.

You can see it in how females love bad boys. Aggression even turns em on rather than terrifies/annoys.

Bad boys get lotsa sex in the era of crumbling families. Everyone knows about girls with no daddies.

When you see a pretty girl you know some guy is putting up with her now.

Hypersexuality is a reproductive strategy to shatter the family, furthered by welfare and feminism.

If you don't do their thing and go to their gatherings they don't wanna see ya: the group's everything.

The fatherless girl doesn't know why she's hyper-sexualized, nor the boy why he's become aggressive.

In war the aggressive male will protect and the hypersexualized girl reproduce: why they choose.

CRUMBLING FAMILIES IS WAR TO THE BRAIN

Crumbling families means war to the biobrain then symptoms roll out of her hypersex and his aggression.

Feminism has created hypersexual females/aggressive males by wrecking family in our recent history.

Never trust a liberal over 3, especially a republican. Ann Coulter

There is a great Determiner who decides the fate of nations.

WORK OR SMIRK

Immaturity is a sort of cognitive impairment: Thinking isn't fully developed, yet they control government?

Altercations are all over politics--there's something about liberty-lovers that erks those thick as bricks.

You know you're superior if their thoughts are just like the club's. Forget these plebs they'll only snub.

Because of what you went through you're now a certain way. From aura to voice they can't take you, ok?

If they don't put you first, hell with em' cuz it hurts the heart and makes everything so much worse.

Science is not determined by majority vote nor consensus, but continual re-evaluation of the facts.

The corrupt military tactic of tyrannies, a disgrace: to deny they're doing it while they do it in your face.

Old guard liberals like Pelosi are still arrogant (doing crazy things) but that'll surely come back to bite em.

Need convalescence after the traumas of life: having to take that from dummies whether husband/wife.

DOUBLE STANDARDS

Conservatives put down for decades. They're seen through negative lens while "loving liberals" get accolades.

A.A. is a liberal social club. I don't see how people stay sober in there/many conservatives feels snubbed.

Liberalism is a mental/spiritual disorder. In the name of tolerance they're the most intolerant, for starters.

Replaced Christian absolutism for cultural relativism and for decades have gone in the opposite direction.

WORK OR SMIRK

A "liberal Christian"is a dangerous, phony and pathetic oxymoron.

There's been a falling away, a drought. The church is a traitor, glad to be out.

Your church is great maybe but there's a falling away generally.

Please grant us patience and fortitude as we plod through these next few days while we wait for our glory raised.

Knowing they're ill allows you to respond (know what's coming) not react (cuz they're so disappointing).

Spiritually ill makes them mentally ill. Sin brings insanity. Repent, symptoms dissolve/you can make a dent.

If you don't know Christian absolutism is right, you'll slide into relativism which is devastation overnight.

Because they're ill they're in denial. They're in denial because they're ill.

Liberals in shock: "Oh no, we're not gonna have any abortions". What a weird, sick and strange reaction.

STING-SHOTS AND FLIP-FLOPS

They always wanna take a pot shot in social gatherings. I'm gonna avoid these stressful dissemblings.

They get you in front of other people and embarrass you. That's the social world, more than I can chew.

Liberals always corrected our speech. They were the superiors, always ready to teach about the breach.

Before Trump we didn't have a comeback. We just accepted what they said and then there was Barrack.

Appeasement always emboldens an aggressor. An aggressor sniffs out weakness and dictators all know her.

Don't argue with them. You now know all about em: adults acting like children and kids echoing.

Their God is their leftist ideology. Without that all hope is gone and about what they did: no apologies.

There's ignorance and apathy, then political correctness creates the perfect storm camouflaged by sympathy.

A constitutional republic is altogether wrong for an immoral people.

Democracy always ends in dictatorship or anarchy. The Founding Fathers never intended that, surely.
Hollywood is licking it's ego wounds like the media. They can't believe you didn't listen to them like idiots.

Actors who can't keep their lives together were convinced they knew better cuz it was on TV to the letter.

They start shooting yelling "Allahu Akbar" and the officials say "we just don't know the motive yet".

It doesn't matter who the shooter is—blame the gun.

See the system: You were compelled to do it but they turned it around/you were blamed/couldn't intuit.

Never have we had more soft, disconnected ivy leaguers running us, always thinking they're better than us.

LIBERTY LOVERS LOVE THE LORD

Rather than being thrilled if someone notices you why not look up to God cuz they don't have a clue!

I love the Lord like most liberty-lovers. We obey only Him and He gives us all great rewards and favor.

Obama didn't go on news with low viewers. He goes on comedy shows with race-bating narratives.

I'm not gonna battle your monitoring of my utterances/political stances cuz you're one of the dunces.

You think it's "nice" to tell people lies all so they'll like you and not see your silly (fake friendly) disguise?

Anything clubby I hate. Unless it's my own club of those who wanna learn about synchronicity/high fate.

The ivy league pseudo-intellectual skinny tie wearers are gonna show you, the bitter clingers.

They're not encroaching nor have anything to do with us but to block Trump let's have a war with Russia.

Brazen, unapologetic corruption.

Mom drummed it into me that men were shit and the best would leave me for a younger woman, omg

"Green" means new taxes.

WITCHCRAFT INTERSECTS FEMINISM

Witchcraft is powerful as intersection of feminism, sexuality, gender, eschewing patriarchy/fight for freedom.

Sign of wickedness: Watch our for anger cuz you will say things and do things that you'll regret later.

Mental transport to another space & time expands the mind. Movies, memories, musing at the sky.

The boomers were the sickest and look what they produced by that BS: a sea of prisons and brokenness.

5G is a weapon system doubling as a communicational system where they can cancer-target dissidents.

Globalization creates the new world then reports it.

WORK OR SMIRK

Above all I gotta manage people's misperceptions, knowing what I know from a life of accusation-frustration.

Forget unnecessary concoctions and recipes except great marinades. Eat what you want: grapes, cheese.

The victory of success is half won when one gains the habit of work then he later get the perks.

They're pejoratively called "holes" but isn't that all they are acting like that? Lol

Work in the early morning then leave the days to muse, think and dream! Don't be stupid/go right-brain.

I pray for your success: ability to remain impervious to the vicissitudes of demographic change.

A shorter more straightforward message rather than getting lost in a big book--vs. a manual for good.

More leisure, more work. Better work, more leisure.

there's a whole nomenclature to this Betrayal Trauma study, like seeing signs here/there--"partial disclosure."

I don't know why, I don't HAVE to know why. There's just too many things pointing to the same pigsty.

FEMINISTS COPY MALE DEBAUCHERY

They trivialize the devastating effects of Playboy on marriages since WWII: Angry feminists seek to copy.

I don't drive, I don't have a cell phone--I just wanna work 18 hours a day and stay in my cozy home!

The democrats wanna pop the bubble to blame Trump then install socialist policies after the slump.

WORK OR SMIRK

Vegans wanna make animal foods incidental in the pyramid and include fake meats as meat-eating is seen as criminal.

I love people (LOL) but nothing's as interesting as being alone.

I was scared and crushed for many years but still knew I deserved it from the fools who I left in tears.

The older I get and the more experience, the bigger the fence.

Rather than recurrently changing diet and announcing it, why not Reverse Diet through time and love it.

Most important criteria for a husband is stability. No kidding, it's not looks or passion but absolute fidelity.

Berries in cream, piece of meat, apple later if hungry--otherwise, nothing until morning and that's daily fasting.

A stable marriage is freedom to the woman. She can become what she wants cuz husband is her fence.

GOOD MARRIAGE IS TOTAL JOY

Marriage cuts out all the crap holding you back. Stable and protected you just become your best in fact.

My major obstacle was people invading me--constantly! They'd never let me work cuz the social came first.

Worst part was people coming over, interrupting my work and plans for the day but a fence made life heavenly.

The sense of bliss when I locked the gate was my home domain where every day's great with refined taste.

Good marriage: every day's a holiday and every meal's a banquet. Warmth and safety like a comfy blanket.

Thru marriage I have freedom/protection to just do my own thing unencumbered by the nuts outside.

Without the stability of marriage you're not impervious to the vicissitudes of demographic change.

The only foods having logic to me are fruit or meats. Dairy too delivered me from vegan deficiencies.

Plants are too fibrous, feeling like a truck in the gut. I'm fiberless now except an apple afternoon snack.

DEALING WITH DEMOGRAPHIC CHANGE

Dealing with demographic change as a single person really sux so find a friend for life whom you can trust.

Public insanity is spreading explosively thru society. Daily we see outbursts in stores and crazy indecency.

People are going insane and such societies are biblical when everyone was mad or deranged in some way.

Mourn a loss of someone by incorporating their best characteristics especially if God came first.

Vegans are globalist pawns. They've been saying for decades they want us off of meat or they make it fake.

Most important thing to have on your desk: raisins. I'm not low carb I'm paleo and breakfast is the reason.

It is amazing the pain women go through for botox. Why not daily fasting to achieve the same results?

NOT eating plants all day long and getting skinny with deficiencies but ONE meal: fat/protein then nothing.

Expert: I need you cuz you know what I need to know and you're the only one who knows what that is.

TRUMPSTERS ARE HATED SO AVOID EM

WORK OR SMIRK

I know! They all hate us cuz we love Trump. But that's a clear indication of who to avoid so don't be bugged.

They can scream and rage at their husbands cuz they're surrounded by women confirmers all around.

Feminism has turned into an ugly, bitter, nasty man-hating horror show but not to pundits "in the know".

Deep thinkers can't tolerate interruptions all day--please stay away.

All of the Muslim countries are 100% Muslim because they won't let you live in peace with them.

It's us against the world but guess Who's on our side?

Think how happy life would be if you never had to argue with another liberal! Now just ignore em--ALL.

Economic freedom and social ethics replaces nation and churches.

An organism can remain true to itself or become a prey to other organisms. I can attest to that, amen.

Freedom of Association and the Right to Exclusion: Constitution says I can associate with you or NOT.

They try to force people on us and MAKE us accept them. That is totally anti-American and totalitarian.

Teens are so communal they think nothing of bringing all their friends to your house, no need to ask.

FORCED US TO BE "SOCIAL" OR INSULT

For decades they've forced us to be "social" upon pain of judgement but no one mentioned independence.

When the whole family are liberals save ONE, what a destiny: He's either goes it alone or leads them home.

WORK OR SMIRK

Kalergi Plan: Mixing up all the races is code for No More White Faces.

It's not that every Muslim is a terrorist but that every terrorist is a Muslim.

Masculinity is toxic? Hell with that: when everything collapses we need men--you didn't know that?

People are too concerned that I be factually accurate rather than morally right. Alexandria Ocasio-Cortez

You can run on for a long time but sooner or later they're gonna cut you down. Johnny Cash song

Do you want to be seduced by the globalists and the high-tech gadgets of the antiChrist, or God?

The Scotch like their meat well-done but the ex-vegan carnivores say it should be all raw plus the blood.

I'm gonna go with my ancestors who were tall and thin centenarians: the meat should be well-done.

When the whole family are liberals save ONE, what a destiny: He either goes it alone or leads em home.

It's you liberals who want open borders--wanting us to be overrun: It's YOU who are the unkind ones.

Bird Box is a pro-white genocide film. A race war is brewing as anyone with senses knows and squirms.

How dirty people have become! Yet we all swim in muddy waters--can't help but get a little on us.

GROOMED AND GLIB CHANGE-MAKERS

Cortez: It's just like Obama--dress him nice/pretty face to SEDUCE THE STUPID so America's debased.

With all due respect you sound so BITTER against this national savior.

Border Wall etc: A fine leader only chokes cuz he listens to what "they" are saying rather than leading.

The more memberships you can claim in oppressed groups, the more aggrieved you are/higher your rank.

The fundamental legal standard is no longer presumption of innocence but believing women always.

An explosion of VMD (Victim Mentality Disorder) has exploded and one symptom is: Making It Up.

Being a "victim" gives authenticity, moral innocence and an aura of admirable courage for surviving it.

It's a RUSH getting a legitimate target for anger while triggering an outpouring of sympathy for female victims.

Complaining about silly things like manspreading but stay quiet in mullticultural deference about raping.

Feminism is so entrenched/men so debased it can only be unraveled through a crisis of massive proportions.

Why was Europe turned into a giant sewer of rape, robbery and death? Because they were sent

Every single night, thousands of cars are burned across Europe--thousands!

How DARE you call convicted murderers "criminals"! Nancy Pelosi

Leftist thinking everywhere even in the churches: "we are all one" BS--causing devastation and mess.

YOU'RE NOT CHOOSING YOU'RE FOLLOWING

You're not choosing you're following a super eugenics-based humanity-ending program, and bragging.

We cannot allow voices like Tucker Carlson to be censored by agenda-driven intimidation efforts. FOX

WORK OR SMIRK

The media isn't "liberal"--it's obedient. Tucker Carlson

Leftist attitude of fascists: their rightness justifies their rudeness.

I found natural rhythm/peak period: It's all night but it begins the day not ends it: start new day 10 p.m.

People who break our laws crossing our borders are more American that you are. Dem view of Americans.

Thru Cortez make it a racial-socialist Hispanic party, bully others to conform-- key demographic locked-in vote.

Cortez is a puppet being loaded information by globalists sitting offshore, taking us to hell and more.

Democrats are a weapon system (sexualizing our children): a demoralization bomb of hellians.

SJWs have taken over the hard sciences too. Even in physics and astronomy the issue is equality, feud.

To a kid the world is a magical place but when waylaid by sex at an early age wonder turns to disgrace.

Marketing: but then creativity takes over and I have no time for the other.

SWEET LIL' LADIES OF THE FIFTIES

Women were sweet lil' ladies in the fifties, supported their husbands/loved em but now told to be shady.

A person who's had a stroke can only do what they do, but I am a conduit and it's beautiful too.

AOL is an absolute tyrant who threatens to arrest people who make fun of her like socialists of the world.

It was a rocky ride, just to write these books I guess. But now I can leave knowing i've done my best.

A society which emasculates it's men will surely be replaced by a society that doesn't. PJ Watson

It's now Pelosi's shutdown. She has decided blocking Trump is more important than America's protection.

Mr. President: Americans are counting on you to not back down! We're sick of chicaneries all around.

All disparity between group outcomes is a direct result of prejudice not IQ or anything else: *Liberal narrative*

Radical egalitarianism flies in the face of a hundred years of iQ testing--who's only answer is "racism".

Despite group averages of dumbness there are brilliant members and idiots among smarts: *facts are no threat!*

RACE REALISM IS NOT RACISM

Race realism, or seeing IQ group averages, is just a FACT and a fact cannot be racist but that's the map.

Most brilliant man who discovered DNA was stripped and banned cuz he told the truth: science is gone.

If they don't understand racial IQ differences they end up hating white people [who musta stole it all}.

The whites will accept slanderous lies more than blacks will accept the truth of racial IQ differences.

A few % points of blacks in America commit over half of the murders in America and that's just facts suh.

The world's not more diverse--we're not going to their countries they're coming here where the money is.

Science is only "correct science" if it always comes out anti-white. Red Ice on James Watson.

WORK OR SMIRK

If all Mexicans went to Japan they'd still be Mexican. If all the Japanese went to Mexico it's still Japan.

There are times when I would like to hang the whole human race and finish the farce. Mark Twain

How do dictators deal with enemies and foes? Bring in multitudes of others given the best land/jobs.

ABOUT YOUR GREAT WORK: PROCEED!

Life didn't work out until I got married (protection). Before then it was hell on earth/a constant invasion.

I feel like a survivor of what people put me through in this life, always invading me/making me unfree.

Freedom is never valued until it is lost, even for a minute. Now I'm so fenced in I'm in bliss and loving it.

It's the person you are, your character and strength, inborn nobility and love of God--that's why you're odd.

I'm not a clinician or a researcher but a theoretician, which is rare. They're the changers, paradigm-aware.

You can make millions but you gotta turn on the engine by keyword optimization.

You're so good it can't help to build up so much it **EXPLODES** and you're rich, famous, renowned but old.

God can make you rich as hell via the internet, His greatest vehicle to get it to me and you, hallelujah!

Tho' they're only 35 pages they may as well be 150 cuz they're so pithy.

BE NEAT, ORDERLY AND ROUTINED

I devote Saturdays to folder clean-up/order and Sundays to keywords/Search Engine Optimization (SEO).

Monday-Friday: Full on creativity from 10 p.m. when I arise to 4 p.m. next day when I lay down to sleep.

It's as if I'm filling in a pre-conceived puzzle as everything fits perfectly and I'm merely God's conduit.
I won't call it automatic writing since that's new age and it's not that--just that I love God as a sage.

Sorry my brain doesn't operate like that. It's dis-abled from conforming and does what it does or it's flat.

I suppose in a tyrannical regime they'd come after me cuz a stroked (unblocked) mind is without inhibitions.

All day long holy sage puts things into place where they belong/removes things that don't, during song.

A genius is simply someone who only wants to work (create) not make money, tho' he needs the latter badly.

DIETARY UPDATES

The further away I get from meat and fat the more I sense violence in my soul. This is re-sensitization.

Dietary update: Fruit smoothie, beans, bread, fast all day. Am I gonna die? I never felt more spry.

I've written on all diets in these books, tried all of em. I'm on lowfat vegan now but could change ag

100 KAREN KELLOCK BOOKS

AFFINITY OR MISERY
AGELESS CORNUCOPIA
AMERICA AWAKE!
AMERICA'S DAFT ERA
ARTS OF PALEO FASTING
AUTOPHAGY ON CHEATERS
BACKSTABBING NEUROTICS
BETRAYAL TRAUMA
BOOMERS AND BROKENNESS
BOOT ON NECK
CHAMPION GUIDES
COMMIE NUTHOUSE
COMMIES
COMMUNIST SPIRIT
CONTAGION OF MADNESS
CONTAGIOUS MADNESS
CULTURE CLASH BASHED
DAFT LEFT
DAILY FASTARIAN
DAM RATS
DIVERSITY IS CRUELTY
E-RACE WHITE
EVIL FREAKS (Beyond Gross)
THE END OR A BEND?
FEMALE BULLIES AND FEMI-NAZIS
FEMALE CARNALITY
FEMALE DUMB DOWN
FEMALE POWER DRIVE
FEMINISM AND RUIN 1 & 2
FIX FOR MISFITS
FOOLS & TRAMPS
FREEDOM SPEAKING
FRENEMY ENABLER
FRENEMY LIAR
FRENEMY THIEF
FRENEMY TRAITOR
TRENEMY TYRANT
GENIUS IS HELD DOWN
GLOBALISLAM
GOD USES THE FLAWED
HAZE OF THE LATTER DAYS

KAREN KELLOCK PH.D.

M.S. Political Science, San Diego State. Ph.D. in Psychology, University of California Irvine. Postdoctoral: UCI School of Medicine, Dept. of Psychiatry [NIMH Grants]. Developed the Debris Theory of Disease, a theory of system pathology in 120 books and 22 textbooks for the general public. The theory has a general formula: All disease is obstruction, all recovery is elimination, all success is attraction. The three obstructions are people, habit and food. Remove obstruction and snap to your goals, waiting in the wings.

www.ingramcontent.com/pod-product-compliance
Lightning Source LLC
Chambersburg PA
CBHW061728250726
48657CB00002B/826